At Issue

| Bitcoin

Other Books in the At Issue Series:

At Issue

Bitcoin

Noah Berlatsky, Book Editor

GREENHAVEN PRESS
A part of Gale, Cengage Learning

GALE
CENGAGE Learning·

Farmington Hills, Mich • San Francisco • New York • Waterville, Maine
Meriden, Conn • Mason, Ohio • Chicago

Patricia Coryell, *Vice President & Publisher, New Products & GVRL*
Douglas Dentino, *Manager, New Products*
Judy Galens, *Acquisitions Editor*

For more information, contact:
Greenhaven Press
27500 Drake Rd.
Farmington Hills, MI 48331-3535
Or you can visit our Internet site at gale.cengage.com

For product information and technology assistance, contact us at

Gale Customer Support, 1-800-877-4253
For permission to use material from this text or product, submit all requests online at www.cengage.com/permissions

Further permissions questions can be e-mailed to permissionrequest@cengage.com

Articles in Greenhaven Press anthologies are often edited for length to meet page requirements. In addition, original titles of these works are changed to clearly present the main thesis and to explicitly indicate the author's opinion. Every effort is made to ensure that Greenhaven Press accurately reflects the original intent of the authors. Every effort has been made to trace the owners of copyrighted material.

Cover image © Imges.com/Corbis.

LIBRARY OF CONGRESS CATALOGING-IN-PUBLICATION DATA

Bitcoin / Noah Berlatsky, book editor.
    pages cm. -- (At issue)
Includes bibliographical references and index.
    ISBN 978-0-7377-7314-9 (hardcover) -- ISBN 978-0-7377-7315-6 (pbk.)
    1. Money. 2. Coinage, International. 3. Tokens. 4. Exchange. 5. Electronic commerce. 6. Virtual reality--Economic aspects. I. Berlatsky, Noah.
    HG221.B5737 2015
    332.4--dc23
                                                              2014030226

Printed in the United States of America
1 2 3 4 5 6 7 18 17 16 15 14

Contents

Introduction

Cryptocurrency is a form of money based on the secure exchange of information. Cryptocurrencies are usually designed so that a certain amount of the currency is created through the solving of algorithms or puzzles. The first cryptocurrency was Bitcoin, developed in 2009, and it remains by far the most popular. However, many other cryptocurrencies have also been developed and put in circulation.

Perhaps the best-known cryptocurrency besides Bitcoin is Litecoin. According to Bloomberg News and *Businessweek* reporter Olga Kharif, litecoin is "cheaper to generate, more plentiful and easier to use for small transactions than bitcoin."[1] Bitcoin mining—solving the puzzles which generate the currency—requires powerful processing equipment. Litecoin, on the other hand, is designed so that it can be mined from regular computers available to most consumers. In addition, the total number of litecoins that can eventually be mined is four times greater than the total number of bitcoins available. The currency's proponents hope that the greater amount of mineable litecoin will make its price lower, thus making it more attractive for use in smaller consumer transactions. Kharif quotes Anton Yemelyanov, one of the developers of litecoin, as saying, "Litecoin has always been viewed as silver to bitcoin's gold. . . . Bitcoin would be used to transact larger value transactions, whereas litecoin would absorb smaller transactional value."[2]

Another challenger to Bitcoin is Dogecoin. This digital currency was begun as something of a joke and retains a light-hearted profile thanks to its mascot, an extremely cute

---

1. Olga Kharif, "Bitcoin Wannabe Litecoin Emerges as Low-Price Challenger," *Bloomberg Businessweek*, April 24, 2014. http://www.businessweek.com/news/2014-04-24/bitcoin -runner-up-litecoin-emerges-as-low-price-challenger-tech.
2. Ibid.

Japanese Shiba Inu dog. The cheerful image could help make Dogecoin popular with younger Internet users, its supporters hope. The coins have initially been used mostly to tip people online who post a good video, or for other small-scale online social transactions. As with Litecoin, Dogecoin is considerably cheaper to mine than Bitcoin: as of May 31, 2014, one bitcoin was worth $529.50, while one dogecoin was worth .059 cents, according to Aaron Crowe in an article on DailyFinance.com. Despite Dogecoin's low-key start, Ben Doernberg, a member of the board of directors of the Dogecoin Foundation, says that eventually "The goal [for Dogecoin] is to actually be *the* online currency."

A third cryptocurrency is Quark, first presented in late 2013. Although it hasn't been around very long, the Quark currency has attracted a good bit of attention because of its "intense security measures,"[4] according to Karis Hustad of the *Christian Science Monitor*. Every transaction with Quark has nine different encryption rounds and six encryption algorithms. It is also supposed to be much faster to mine Quark than to mine other currencies, and (like Litecoin and Dogecoin) each quark is worth a relatively small amount, so it is more convenient than Bitcoin for small purchases.

There are numerous other cryptocurrencies as well. Peercoin, for example, is similar to Bitcoin but has controls in place to make it harder for any one person or group to monopolize the mining of the currency. Namecoin is both a currency and a decentralized Internet address—which means that, when you get a namecoin, you also get a domain name which is outside the regular Internet. Infinitecoin is similar to Litecoin but has the potential to generate more than one thousand times more coins through mining. And then there's

---

4. Karis Hustad, "Sick of Mt. Gox and Bitcoin? Here Are Four Alternative Cryptocurrencies," *Christian Science Monitor*, February 26, 2014. http://www.csmonitor.com /Business/2014/0226/Sick-of-Mt.-Gox-and-Bitcoin-Here-are-four-alternative -cryptocurrencies.

Megacoin and Novacoin and Feathercoin and more according to Samuel Gibbs of the British newspaper *The Guardian*.

Obviously, cryptocurrencies are hot, and there are many tech folks who enjoy inventing them and figuring out new ways to make trickier and better currencies with new and exciting features. The question remains, however, will anyone actually use them? Money is only useful as money if it is widely accepted and circulated. There are only a very limited number of stores or vendors who will accept payment in bitcoins. Finding someone to accept payment in litecoin is going to be even more difficult. And what are the chances of finding even one business that will accept feathercoin as payment? It's not clear whether Bitcoin will ever gain sufficient widespread acceptance to actually be a viable form of money, much less the dozens of wannabe bitcoins that have emerged since Bitcoin's introduction. As Adam Draper, an investor in Bitcoin startups, told Olga Kharif for her *Businessweek* article, "Alternative currencies are great. . . . They all run into the same problem, though. They are not Bitcoin."[5]

At Issue: Bitcoin looks at other controversies around Bitcoin, including such issues as whether the currency should be banned, whether it should be regulated, whether it favors the wealthy over the poor, and whether it is a real currency.

5. Op. cit.

1

An Explanation of Bitcoin

Adam Serwer and Dana Liebelson

Adam Serwer is a former reporter at Mother Jones *who has also written for* The Washington Post, *the* Village Voice, *and other publications. Dana Liebelson is a reporter in* Mother Jones's *Washington bureau who has also written for* Marie Claire *and* The Week.

Bitcoin is an electronic currency that appeals to people who want their anonymity protected, or who don't want banks or governments involved in their online transactions. Much about Bitcoin is uncertain at this point, including how or whether it will be regulated and even how a person can exchange money for bitcoins.

What is a Bitcoin? How did you pay for your coffee this morning, by cash? By credit card? If a growing number of bank-fearing techies have their way, you'll soon be able to pay for that mocha latte through an untraceable virtual currency called Bitcoin. As of this month, Bitcoins are worth over a billion dollars, and interest in the currency is skyrocketing. Here's everything you need to know about a currency that sounds like it belongs in a fantastical realm: You can't touch it, it's prized in the underworld, its creator disappeared in a cloud of mystery, and if you want to keep it safe, you should keep it hidden in a bunch of different places.

What Is It?

No, but really. What is it? A Bitcoin is a unit of currency, launched in 2009, that only exists online and isn't controlled by any kind of central authority, like the US Federal Reserve. You can send Bitcoins to anyone who has a web connection (or hand someone your hard drive containing the currency.) You hold on to Bitcoins by setting up a virtual wallet, either through a third-party website, or by storing it on software run on your computer—although storing your Bitcoin wallet only on your computer is about as secure as stuffing hundred-dollar bills under your mattress. As soon as you have your wallet, you're part of the big Bitcoin network. If you want to buy something from your neighbor, you simply need to obtain their anonymous identification number and send them some Bitcoins, which takes between 15 minutes and an hour to process. . . .

There have been incidents where Bitcoin users have illicitly attempted to use other people's computers to mine Bitcoins.

What is a Bitcoin wallet? A Bitcoin wallet is a service that holds your Bitcoins for you. Unlike banks, Bitcoin wallet firms don't generally invest the money you deposit with them. But there's a catch—Bitcoin wallets don't have the Federal Deposit Insurance Corporation [FDIC] backing that insures Americans' bank deposits up to $100,000. "There's no such thing as FDIC insurance when it comes to Bitcoin," says Reuben Grinberg, an attorney at Davis Polk & Wardwell who specializes in financial matters and wrote an early legal analysis of Bitcoin. If your Bitcoin wallet gets robbed or collapses, you're out of luck. . . .

Why Bitcoin?

Why do people use Bitcoin?

Bitcoin appeals to people who are suspicious of financial institutions and central banks like the US Federal Reserve. "There are types like me, libertarian gold-buggish folks," for whom "inflation is a constant worry" and who "see the cryptography in Bitcoin as insulation against inflation," explains Jim Harper, the director of information policy studies at the Cato Institute. People seeking privacy in their financial transactions—for legitimate or illegitimate reasons—might also use Bitcoin because it's more anonymous than financial transactions using credit or debit cards. "A lot of these people who have a deep distrust of government are really interested in anonymity and autonomy. They want to keep the government out of their business," Grinberg says. "In a lot of these people's minds, governments will come and go, financial instruments will disappear, you could have anarchy, but Bitcoin will be here to stay." As with gold, the idea is that the value of Bitcoin could survive some sort of cataclysm. The value of Bitcoin isn't actually very stable however, so that may not be a good bet.

Where do Bitcoins come from? New Bitcoins are created in a process called "mining," which involves Bitcoin users attempting to figure out a complex mathematical solution related to the current number of Bitcoins. Grinberg compares it to finding the missing piece of a puzzle. Whomever finds the puzzle piece wins a certain number of Bitcoins, and the process starts all over again. Finding the Bitcoin solution involves an incredible amount of processing power, and so users often band together in "pools" in order to find the solution and to earn Bitcoins more regularly. However, there have been incidents where Bitcoin users have illicitly attempted to use other people's computers to mine Bitcoins. You can do this by hacking people's computers and telling them to mine Bitcoins. In one incident referenced by the FBI, a system administrator at a university in New York set its computers to mine Bitcoins for him.

Is Bitcoin legal? In the United States, the answer is probably yes, but it could depend on what state you're in. Doing something illegal with Bitcoins—like bribing someone or buying drugs—is still illegal.

Bitcoin Value

How much is a Bitcoin worth?

In August 2012, the exchange rate for 1 Bitcoin was about $10. When Kevin Roose of *New York* magazine wrote about buying a Bitcoin on April 4, [2013], the price was at $140. And as of Tuesday night, April 10, it's up to $234. It's not clear why, but Harper says the rapid price rise could be attributed to anything from increased media attention to concern surrounding the financial crisis in Cyprus, where bank accounts were going to be taxed to finance a bailout of the island nation's financial sector.

How many Bitcoins are there? The Bitcoin foundation states that there will never be more than 21 million Bitcoins at a time. That could create a problem for the currency, however, because people might sit on their Bitcoins rather than buy things with them, hoping that they appreciate in value.

What can you buy with them?

If you earn income with your Bitcoins, you technically still have to pay taxes on them.

You can buy anything from any company that accepts Bitcoins as currency. There aren't that many of them. However, privacy activists have lauded the ability of Bitcoins to preserve the anonymity of political dissidents to publish online in countries where Internet access is restricted. The Freedom of the Press Foundation says that Bitcoin "offers the potential for a censorship-resistant currency." One of the more popular uses for Bitcoin, however, seems to be the purchase of illegal drugs, because like cash the transactions are harder to trace, but unlike cash, they can take place over long distances. "When you're talking about normal American consumers, is there anything legal they can get with Bitcoins that they can't get with dollars or with their credit card?" Grinberg says. "I think the answer is no."

Criminal Uses

Why do people say Bitcoins are easier for criminals to use?

Bitcoins provide a certain amount of anonymity for users, because the accounts are just numbers and not necessarily linked to an individual identity. You can also create a new wallet for each new Bitcoin transaction, further hiding your identity. But it's not completely anonymous, says Grinberg. Bitcoin users who reveal information to third parties, either a Bitcoin wallet provider or even through joining pools to mine Bitcoins, are making it more likely their identities could be discovered. But because all Bitcoin transactions are public, it's theoretically possible that you could use the account numbers to discover someone's identity. "It's possible that using statistical techniques and information that's publicly available you could find out a great deal about Bitcoin users," Grinberg says. Also if you're using a third-party Bitcoin wallet, the feds have a number of ways to compel corporations to reveal user information when it comes to matters of national security.

Can you use Bitcoin to avoid taxes? Yes, in the same way you could use cash to avoid taxes. The more that people use Bitcoin this way, however, the more likely that governments will get better at finding people who do so. "Just like people who accept cash, it's generally easier to evade taxes," says Grinberg, "but as a large-scale tool to evade taxes," he's "not sure" it would work. If you earn income with your Bitcoins, you technically still have to pay taxes on them.

Can they be hacked?

Bitcoin wallets and exchanges can be hacked. "There's plenty of stories where Bitcoin exchanges have been hacked," says Cato's Harper. "One of the weaknesses of Bitcoin by far is that people don't know very well how to secure their Bitcoin." Of course, identities can be stolen and regular bank accounts hacked too.

Will Bitcoins ever replace national currencies? That seems like a long shot right now.

Which famous people use Bitcoins?

Ashton Kutcher's venture capital firm, A-Grade Investments, invested in a Bitcoin pay network, according to Beta Beat. And *BuzzFeed* speculates that there has to be at least a few Bitcoin millionaires, although they only managed to track down a Reddit user claiming to be one. So if celebrities are using Bitcoins, they're not bragging about it. Who should be the next Bitcoin celebrity spokesperson? Users in this Bitcoin forum note that Sean Penn, Charlie Sheen, President Obama, and the woman who "works for Fox Sports and also plays the character 'Chelsea' on TNA Wrestling on Spike TV" would all make good candidates.

Regulation

What does Obama say? The Treasury Department released a statement in March [2013] saying that certain entities—but not the average Bitcoin user—may have to register with Fin-CEN, the wing of the Treasury Department that deals with financial crimes and money laundering. "Someone who mines some Bitcoins and then uses them to buy goods or services, and not as part of business—would likely not have to register," Grinberg says. "However, once you move beyond that minimal level of involvement in the Bitcoin world," like setting up a Bitcoin exchange, you might have to register. Grinberg says it's still not entirely clear what the rules are yet.

Will Bitcoins ever replace national currencies? That seems like a long shot right now. "There's enough to be cautious about with Bitcoin that I don't see whole countries abandoning their currency and using Bitcoin," Harper says, although he argues that Bitcoin could be useful to people in countries without a stable currency. "It doesn't bring us to libertarian Shangri-La or anarcho-capitalism or anything like that."

Is Bitcoin going to bring down the world financial system? Probably not. "It's still a drop in the bucket in terms of the world economy," Grinberg says. "It's not crazy to think it might go much higher and that its market cap might become so large to exert some influence on, if not the world economy, the local economies where it starts getting used more."

Who invented Bitcoin? Bitcoin's founder is Satoshi Nakamoto, which is a pseudonym. Nakamoto "released Bitcoin to the world at the beginning of 2009, but said he had been working on it since 2007," explains Gavin Andresen, whom Nakamoto made coadministrator of the software when he left the project. The idea was mentioned before that, but Jon Holmquist, head of marketing at BitcoinStore.com, says Nakamoto was responsible for combining and solidifying the ideas into a practical paper. Both Andresen and his colleague say they have "no idea" of the founder's real identity. Nakamoto's alleged profile on P2P Foundation claims that he is a 38-year-old male living in Japan, although that has been met with skepticism, given his strong command of American English.

Buying Bitcoins

How do I convert dollars to Bitcoins?

There are a number of ways to convert dollars to Bitcoins, but as Grinberg notes, "it's not straightforward" for the average person, and "even the 'easy' version is hard." Also, if you live in a rural area, or have qualms about handing over all of your bank information to an anonymous internet stranger, then you might want to just give up now. The major Bitcoin exchanges don't accept credit cards—because of that whole anonymity problem—so instead, you're encouraged to purchase Bitcoins by adding your bank account information to a site like Coinbase, and transferring money that way. You can also get Bitcoins by using your phone, the virtual program Second Life, wire transfer, or at a cash deposit location like CVS. Bitcoin users caution against PayPal—because it might freeze your account—and say that "buying Bitcoins in person can be fun and safe!" . . .

In which other countries can you buy Bitcoins? Canada, Mexico, Argentina, Brazil, parts of the European Union, the United Kingdom, Russia and Malaysia, to start. *Mother Jones* asked Andresen whether you could buy Bitcoins with, say, the Indonesian rupiah, and he said that "I don't know if there is an exchange from Indonesian currency to Bitcoins yet."

Will Bitcoins ever be used by banks? Many users like Bitcoin precisely because they see it as an alternative to putting their money in banks. But it's possible that more traditional banking institutions using Bitcoin could pop up at some point.

2

Bitcoin Points to the Future of Cryptocurrency

Molly Wood

Molly Wood is an executive editor at CNET, author of the Molly Rants *blog, and host of the tech show* Always On.

Bitcoin is an important step forward in the field of cryptocurrency. Some have suggested that Bitcoin is insecure, or that it is just a tech fad. However, the truth is that Bitcoin is quite secure, difficult to hack, and protected from bank robberies, which are more common than many people realize. Technological advances, such as the Internet, have become central to the economy, and government interest in Bitcoin suggests that the currency, or a currency like it, is likely to become important in the future.

The interesting thing about Bitcoin isn't what it is today. What's interesting is that this experiment is turning into a serious proving ground for the idea of "crypto-currency," digitally created currency protected by powerful cryptography.

Crypto-currency is traceable, more portable than paper money, and harder to steal. If the Bitcoin experiment proves successful, how soon will a government or other regime develop, back, and distribute crypto-currency as a true alternative currency?

My money, paper or virtual, says that day is coming.

A particularly evolved regime could officially back a crypto-currency, issue some basic standards and regulations for use, and then continue to allow it to be community mined and distributed. You'd get the security benefits of decentralized production, the peer-to-peer buy-in of a barter currency, and none of the printing costs or insecurity of paper.

On the other hand, a particularly devolved regime could do all those things but use the digital power of the currency to spy on its users, control or corrupt the flow of currency, or implement the tech insecurely and disrupt the global economy. A major move to crypto-currency could go either way, but I bet it's coming, nevertheless.

First, let's get past the crypto-currency and Bitcoin objections. This technology is here to stay—so let's take the arguments point by point.

What About the Gold Standard?

The first objection to Bitcoin, of course, is that it isn't backed by anything, so despite a trust and barter system, it's ultimately worthless. Let's be honest: The reason people are interested in alternative currencies in the first place is that it sometimes feels like the paper in your wallet and certainly the plastic are equally ephemeral.

A crypto-currency may be hackable, but it can also be really, really, really *hard to hack—harder than robbing a bank.*

But let's assume we're talking about a centrally issued crypto-currency of the future: Problem solved. Backing would be ensured, but mining and distribution could remain decentralized to promote better security and code innovation.

It's Insecure: Anything Can Be Hacked

Yes, anything can be hacked. But it's worth noting that Bitcoin *itself* has never been hacked. In fact, famed hacker Dan Kaminsky said he tried to hack it and failed. Some of the technologies *around* Bitcoin, including some of the exchange sites, have been hacked, but never the actual currency algorithms.

And paper money is also insecure. Thanks to a huge, fast-moving, and occasionally corrupt electronic trading market, billions can be lost in errant keystrokes, false tweets, or simple fraud. Plus, there are still good old-fashioned bank robberies: Did you know most people who rob banks actually get away with it? Not exactly confidence-building.

A crypto-currency may be hackable, but it can also be *really, really, really* hard to hack—harder than robbing a bank. And if mining and exchanges remain decentralized despite a central backing body, you'll see hacks that may sound major but actually do minor damage to the entire currency pool. Plus, digital currency has traceable transactions. It can even have traceable code embedded during the mining process. So to discourage or respond to theft, a regime could blacklist or poison stolen currency, rendering it useless and possibly even using blacklisted code to find thieves.

Bitcoin proper isn't likely to come with a blacklisting scheme. It's unregulated and blacklisting would be tricky at best—its community would have to agree on a set of standards that would trigger poisoning specific coins. It could end up punishing innocent users, and it can be technically difficult to track stolen coins, thanks to services called "mixers" that mix coin code and effectively launder Bitcoins.

But blacklisting is still technically possible; it's quite easy to imagine a centrally issued crypto-currency having a set of standards and chain-blocking to both trace stolen currency and prevent its use.

To be clear, I'm not advocating this usage, and there are plenty of good arguments against it, but I can imagine it being appealing to banks and governments that might decide that security and currency tracking are more valuable than fungibility.[1]

---

1. Fungibility means that individual units of a currency can be substituted for other units of equal value, so if you owe $10, it doesn't matter which specific $10 bill you pay with.

It's Just a Techie Experiment

It's easy to dismiss Bitcoin or crypto-currencies as the flailings of a disaffected, semi-anarchist hacker community trying to undermine the system. But you know what? Hackers created the Internet, and the decidedly anti-establishment Steve Jobs [founder of Apple] gave us the modern technology era we know and love today. A lot of good ideas started out as techie experimentation. Plus, and more saliently, I have it on good authority that the U.S. government and others are very, very interested in Bitcoin—so much so that there are nascent attempts to regulate it and federal authorities and lawmakers have been warning about its nefarious nature for a couple of years now.

Crypto-currency is a certifiable Pretty Big Deal. The Facebook antagonists otherwise known as the Winklevoss twins[2] have amassed huge sums of Bitcoin; it's minting its own millionaires (in real dollars); and an increasing number of global citizens consider Bitcoin a better investment than Wall Street these days.

You don't have to buy it—literally or figuratively—but Bitcoin is already changing the world, and I have a feeling the real changes are just beginning.

---

2. The Winklevoss twins are American rowers and Internet entrepreneurs. They sued Facebook claiming it stole their original social networking idea.

3

Bitcoin Is Insecure and Overhyped

Jim Edwards

Jim Edwards is a reporter for Business Insider *and former managing editor for* Adweek. *He has also written for* Salon, MTV, The Nation, *and AOL.com.*

Bitcoin proponents claim that the currency is more secure than other currencies. However, there have been numerous bitcoin thefts; many sites have been hacked, and many users have lost substantial amounts of money. Again, Bitcoin proponents say that the sites can be hacked but that Bitcoin itself cannot be, by which they mean people cannot create false bitcoins. The stability of the currency, however, is itself a security threat, since it means that once bitcoins are moved, the transaction cannot be reversed. The federal government does not back or insure Bitcoin the way it backs traditional bank transactions.

One of the most powerful myths about Bitcoin—the encrypted, independent online currency that's become a huge trend in recent months—is that Bitcoin is "secure."

Not Secure

Bitcoin.org, the semi-official voice of the Bitcoin community, says "the whole system is protected by heavily peer-reviewed cryptographic algorithms like those used for online banking.

No organization or individual can control Bitcoin, and the network remains secure even if not all of its users can be trusted."

But Bitcoin is not secure.

There have been dozens of robberies of Bitcoin banks and exchanges, and millions of dollars have been lost.

To put that in perspective, if robbers were routinely walking into brick-and-mortar banks and taking millions of dollars, with zero consequences and no arrests, it would make huge headlines every day. The media would be on high alert for the next heist.

But on the Internet, Bitcoin thefts worth hundreds of thousands and millions of dollars happen on a weekly basis and no one cares.

Robberies

Here are a few recent examples of Bitcoin robberies, and then we'll explain why Bitcoin is not 100% "secure."

- The Chinese Bitcoin GBL went offline earlier this month, [November 2013] taking $4.1 million in users' accounts with it.

- In Australia, a Bitcoin exchange run by an 18-year-old user named "Tradefortress," claims to have lost $1 million of his users' money.

- Also in November, a Czech exchange, Bitcash.cz, declared that hackers had made off with an undisclosed amount stored in its users' Bitcoin wallets.

- In September, Bitfloor announced that it had lost $250,000 in hacked Bitcoins.

- Last year $228,845 was stolen from a trading platform known as Bitcoinica.

Perhaps the biggest heist was pulled off by the U.S. government. After Ross Ulbricht, the alleged "Dread Pirate Roberts" who ran the online drugs market Silk Road was arrested by the FBI, authorities reported they had seized nearly $29 million in Bitcoins controlled by him. Techdirt later noted that some of the money may have belonged to users who did business on his site, and not all the business transacted there was illegal.

Bitcoin is vulnerable in the same way any other online asset is vulnerable.

Don't hold your breath for refunds.

Here's a website devoted to listing dozens of Bitcoin robberies through 2012 [bitcointalk.org]. In 2011, Ars Technica reported on this description of what it is like to be the victim of Bitcoin theft:

> The user known as "allinvain" is a long-time contributor to the Bitcoin forums. He says he's been mining Bitcoins for over a year, and had amassed a fortune of 25,000 BTC. This was a modest sum a few months ago, when Bitcoins were worth pennies, but over the last two months the value of a Bitcoin skyrocketed to around $20, which means 25,000 BTC would have been worth half a million dollars. "I remember watching the price like a hawk," he wrote.
>
> And then disaster struck. "I just woke up to see a very large chunk of my bitcoin balance gone," he wrote. "Needles [sic] to say I feel like I have lost faith in bitcoin." He speculated that a Windows security flaw may have allowed the culprit to gain access to his digital wallet. "I feel like killing myself now," he said.

Bitcoin is vulnerable in the same way any other online asset is vulnerable: Passwords can be stolen or guessed, accounts can be hacked. Most of the thefts involve hacking into users' accounts. Bitfloor's description of how it lost $250,000 in Bitcoin is typical. A hacker found an unencrypted copy of the coded keys to users' wallets:

> Last night, a few of our servers were compromised. As a result, the attacker gained accesses to an unencrypted backup of the wallet keys (the actual keys live in an encrypted area). Using these keys they were able to transfer the coins. This attack took the vast majority of the coins BitFloor was holding on hand. As a result, I have paused all exchange operations.

In fact, Bitcoin defenders say this is exactly the point. Bitcoin isn't insecure—you are!

Once a Bitcoin transaction has been approved by both sides, it cannot be reversed without the permission of the recipient. So when hackers engineer the transaction, the cash is gone forever.

Here's Bitcoin.org's answer to that very question on security:

> Although these events are unfortunate, none of them involve Bitcoin itself being hacked, nor imply inherent flaws in Bitcoin; just like a bank robbery doesn't mean that the dollar is compromised. However, it is accurate to say that a complete set of good practices and intuitive security solutions is needed to give users better protection of their money, and to reduce the general risk of theft and loss.

The idea that Bitcoin is "secure" even though it can be stolen is a bit like saying that gold is "secure," even if it is being spirited away by gangsters. They can't *destroy* the gold, after all.

Not Reversible

What they really mean is that Bitcoins themselves cannot be copied or faked, like counterfeit bills. Anyone receiving a Bitcoin can be confident that it is real and valuable.

But that aspect of its security—the permanence of the value in the transaction—turns out to be Bitcoin's biggest security flaw. Once a Bitcoin transaction has been approved by both sides, it cannot be reversed without the permission of the recipient. So when hackers engineer the transaction, the cash is gone forever.

That's *not* what happens with traditional currency. In the U.S., if your bank is robbed or even if the bank goes out of business, the FDIC backs up the lost deposits and replaces your money, up to $250,000 per bank.

And then there is this new theory from Cornell University which posits that there is an incentive in the system for users to cooperate and hoard their coins until they control a majority of available Bitcoins. At that point, the currency collapses.

Bitcoin is only as "secure" as the fallible, ill-intentioned users who open accounts, create passwords and covet their fellows' wallets.

Which is to say, not especially secure.

4

Bitcoin Is Doomed Because Transactions Are Irreversible

Nicholas Weaver

Nicholas Weaver is a researcher at the International Computer Science Institute in Berkeley, California, and University of California San Diego.

Bitcoin transactions cannot be reversed, which means that there is no way to rectify theft or fraud once it is completed. That makes Bitcoin inherently risky. Bitcoin storage locations can be hacked, which means that it is dangerous to have a Bitcoin wallet connected to any Internet device. There is no cheap, efficient way to buy bitcoins; transactions instead require cash and in many cases personal meetings. Bitcoin is inconvenient and subject to theft, and it will never become a fully functioning currency.

Bitcoin is the world's most popular digital currency—not just a form of money, but a way of moving money around—and the darling topic *du jour* of the tech industry right now. . . .

As a security researcher, I admire bitcoin-the-protocol. But I believe bitcoin-the-currency contains a fatal flaw.

Fatal Flaw

As a security researcher, I admire bitcoin-the-protocol. It's an incredibly clever piece of cryptographic engineering, especially the proof-of-work as a way of maintaining an indelible history and a signature scheme which, when properly used, can limit the damage that might be done by an adversary with a quantum computer. But I believe bitcoin-the-currency contains a fatal flaw, one that ensures that bitcoin won't ever achieve widespread adoption as a currency.

The flaw? That bitcoin transactions are irreversible. That is, they can never be undone: Once committed, there is no "oops", no "takeback", no "control-Z". Combined with bitcoin's independence—it is a separate currency with a floating exchange rate—this flaw is arguably lethal to money systems.

Bitcoin advocates will argue that both its irreversibility and independence are benefits. That they were explicit design decisions to defy control by governments or banks. But to me these features are flaws, because a tenet of modern finance asserts that anything electronic must be reversible. If bitcoin really is the internet applied to money . . . then it, too, should have a "back" button.

Without an undo/back button, it's only possible to *prevent* fraud. With an undo, it would also be possible to *detect and mitigate* fraud; to see that something bad happened and then actually do something about it. Credit cards, bank account transfers, and all other electronic transactions involving a bank all have an "undo" button.

What sort of online currency requires using offline computers and objects for all storage?

Banks rely on the reversibility feature every day to stop fraudulent activities. Bitcoin robbery cases aren't just rising because of interest in the currency—the most recent is a European bitcoin payment processor losing $1M after a DDoS [denial of service] attack—they're rising because robbing a bank online involves much less friction than doing so in person.

Bitcoin Theft Is Easy

In the current financial system, the only major irreversible transactions involve withdrawing cash. This is a process that must happen in person and therefore naturally imposes substantial limits; in-person requirements provide attribution, keep an attacker from automating the process, and limit the "attack surface." For example:

- To steal a million dollars hidden under mattresses, a thief needs to break into thousands of homes.

- To steal a million dollars from a typical business's bank account, thieves need to transfer it to a network of roughly 100 money mules.

- Each mule must then withdraw less than $10,000 from their account within a short period of time, take the cash to Western Union, and wire the money to the thieves. (This is why those running the mules can claim up to 40–50 percent of the take!)

To steal a million dollars worth of bitcoins stored by a business, however, a thief only needs the private key. Likewise, to steal $1000 worth of bitcoins each from 1000 people, the thief only needs to have his or her bot software running on enough victims with enough bitcoins to automate the process.

This means bitcoins *should never be "stored" on an internet-connected device.* That includes our computers and our smartphones. (And have you heard the one about the guy who keeps his key on his finger?) Let's pause for a moment to reflect on that: What sort of online currency requires using offline computers and objects for all storage?

Blocking Bitcoins

Now, it is theoretically true that stolen coins could be blocked. If a portion of the network blocks stolen bitcoins today, then the same mechanism could block bitcoins that passed through black markets or offshore exchanges (such as BTC-e) that don't implement anti-money-laundering protections. Yet the bitcoin community strongly resists the idea of blacklists, because it eliminates fungibility—the notion that all bitcoins are identical—which is essential for a currency. If every dollar used in a drug deal couldn't be used again, would dollars work as currency? Especially if, sometime after acceptance, a dollar becomes void and blacklisted after the fact because of its previous involvement in a crime?

Bitcoin advocates insist that the theft problem is solvable. For the sake of argument, let's assume that some bitcoin-centric hardware company deploys completely secure and free hardware bitcoin wallets for anyone to use. And let's also assume consumers are happy with such an unregulatable model and don't care that merchants can now rip them off with near impunity. Immunity from theft is not enough. Irreversibility, combined with volatility, ensures that bitcoin still will never see wide adoption.

To actually buy something with the "digital currency of the future" . . . the buyer has to go to the bank, withdraw cash, turn it into bitcoins, and then spend it quickly.

Bitcoin's irreversibility means that a bitcoin exchange can *never* accept credit cards or wire transfers to quickly provide bitcoins in significant quantities. These agencies must carefully audit customers, wait on any large purchases, and assign blame when attackers breach accounts. Any exchange that does not follow such precautions would be a magnet for fraud, and cease to exist once they start receiving chargebacks.

As a consequence, the only ways to *quickly* buy bitcoins require cash—again, I'm talking about convenience here which surely should be a feature of internet applied to money. This convenience can happen via a cash drop at a drugstore; a cash deposit into the *exchange's* bank account; a face-to-face meetup; or at an actual ATM, complete with cameras and withdrawal limits. (The world's first bitcoin ATM just went live a month ago in Canada. Incidentally, it takes cash, not ATM cards.)

And almost every bitcoin purchase needs to start with such a consuming, hastle-prone step if the buyer is unwilling to risk the wild swings in value that bitcoin experiences on a day-to-day basis. Since bitcoin has no stable value, the recipient should immediately go the other way. After all, if bitcoin's volatility is desired by the merchant, they can just buy bitcoins independently. Instead, any sensible merchant receiving them will immediately turn them back into Dollars, Euros, or whatever local currency they need at a cost of roughly 1 percent. Which means the buyer first had to go the other way, turning dollars into bitcoins. Otherwise, the system would be out of balance.

Thus to actually buy something with the "digital currency of the future"—without having to wait, have funds predeposited at an exchange, or risk that one's bitcoins drop in value— the buyer has to go to the bank, withdraw cash, turn it into bitcoins, and then spend it quickly.

In the greater scheme of things, bitcoin is small: even at a roughly 10 billion dollar market capitalization it is almost irrelevant in financial terms.

Bitcoin Requires Cash

The need to go in person and withdraw cash conservatively costs the buyer 2 percent, as gas stations can charge over 2 percent to accept credit cards (and yet, people regularly use credit over cash). For reference, compare this to Square, which charges 2.75 percent to process credit cards. So even if you *can* conveniently get bitcoins from your local ATM—though we're nowhere near there yet—a bitcoin transaction will cost the buyer and seller a combined 3 percent or more.

Even the much-vaunted international transfer use case doesn't make sense here: A bitcoin transaction may be cheaper than a SWIFT wire transfer, but the cash requirement means it is not necessarily cheaper than Western Union. (To Mexico, it's $8 plus a currency exchange fee. Europe is far more expensive, but that's due to a lack of competition rather than something intrinsic.) If Western Union charges nearly double the currency conversion fee of a bitcoin exchange, it still comes out approximately the same since a foreign bitcoin transaction involves two currency exchanges rather than one.

Bitcoin therefore only works for merchants who face substantial chargebacks but who can't say "pay cash", are selling to bitcoin believers willing to pay the premium price to use bitcoins, or want to conduct business that the credit card system blocks. Yet many of the transactions blocked by the credit card system—namely gambling, drugs, and crypto-extortion—are themselves illegal. In those cases, does it really make sense to use such an innately traceable currency with a permanent record? I think not. (You can bet that redandwhite, the "hitman" Dread Pirate Roberts allegedly hired, is going to be asking himself that question over the coming months.)

This is not to say that bitcoin won't retain its price. After all, the greater-sucker theory of speculation can ensure a large price for a long period. As long as bitcoin believers can recruit enough new money to balance the newly mined-for-sale coins, the price may sustain itself indefinitely. And, in the greater scheme of things, bitcoin is small: even at a roughly 10 billion dollar market capitalization it is almost irrelevant in financial terms. This is probably roughly the peak market capitalization achieved by Beanie Babies in 1999.

There are indeed important and valuable ideas that exist in bitcoin's design. But bitcoin itself? I believe its volatility and built-in irreversibility will doom it to the ash-heap of history.

5

Bitcoin Transactions Are Reversible

Eli Dourado

Eli Dourado is a research fellow at the Mercatus Center at George Mason University with the Technology Policy Program. He studies and writes about issues like Internet governance, intellectual property, cybersecurity, and cryptocurrency through the lens of political economy.

Critics of Bitcoin argue that the transactions are not reversible. By this they mean that if you make a payment and goods are not delivered, you cannot get your money back, as you can with a credit card payment. However, Bitcoin does in fact have a system for making transactions reversible. Bitcoin provides a system whereby transactions can be monitored by an arbiter, who can return bitcoins to an injured party in the case of fraud. Few people have used the arbitration aspects of Bitcoin yet, but they offer exciting possibilities for financial innovation involving the transaction of bitcoins.

One of the criticisms leveled at Bitcoin by those people determined to hate it is that Bitcoin transactions are irreversible. If I buy goods from an anonymous counterparty online, what's to stop them from taking my bitcoins and simply not sending me the goods? When I buy goods online using Visa or American Express, if the goods never arrive, or if they aren't what was advertised, I can complain to the credit card

Eli Dourado, "Stop Saying Bitcoin Transacations Aren't Reversible," elidourado.com (blog), December 4, 2013. www.elidourado.com. Copyright © 2013 by Eli Dourado. All rights reserved. Reproduced with permission.

company. The company will do a cursory investigation, and if they find that I was indeed likely ripped off, they will refund me my money. Credit card transactions are reversible, Bitcoin transactions are not. For this service (among others), credit card companies charge merchants a few percentage points on the transaction.

Arbitrators

The problem with this account is that it's not true: Baked into the Bitcoin protocol, there is support for what are known as "m-of-n" or "multisignature" transactions, transactions that require some number *m* out of some higher number *n* parties to sign off.

The simplest variant is a 2-of-3 transaction. Let's say that I want to buy goods online from an anonymous counterparty. I transfer money to an address jointly controlled by me, the counterparty, and a third-party arbitrator (maybe even Amex). If I get the goods, they are acceptable, and I am honest, I sign the money away to the seller. The seller also signs, and since 2 out of 3 of us have signed, he receives his money. If there is a problem with the goods or if I am dishonest, I sign the bitcoins back to myself and appeal to the arbitrator. The arbitrator, like a credit card company, will do an investigation, make a ruling, and either agree to transfer the funds back to me or to the merchant; again, 2 of 3 parties must agree to transfer the funds.

This is *not* an escrow service; at no point can the arbitrator abscond with the funds. The arbitrator is paid a market rate in advance for his services, which are offered according to terms agreed upon by all three parties. This is *better* than the equivalent service using credit cards, because credit cards rely on huge network effects and consequently there are only a handful of suppliers of such transaction arbitration. Using Bitcoin, *anyone* can be an abitrator, including the traditional credit card companies (although they might have to lower their fees). Competition in both terms and fees is likely to result in better discovery of efficient rules for dispute resolution.

While multisignature transactions are not well understood, they are right there in the Bitcoin protocol, as much a valid Bitcoin transaction as any other. So *some* Bitcoin transactions are irreversible; others *are* reversible, exactly as reversible as credit card transactions are.

What excites me most about the decentralized arbitration afforded by multisignature transactions is that it could be the beginnings of a Common Law for the Internet.

Financial Innovation

Bitrated.com is a new site (announced yesterday on Hacker News) that facilitates setting up multisignature transactions. Bitcoin client support for multisignature transactions is limited, so the site helps create addresses that conform to the m-of-n specifications. At no point does the site have access to the funds in the multisignature address.

In addition, Bitrated provides a marketplace where people can advertise their arbitration services. Users are able to set up transactions using arbitrators both from the site or from anywhere else. The entire project is open source, so if you want to set up a competing directory, go for it.

What excites me most about the decentralized arbitration afforded by multisignature transactions is that it could be the beginnings of a Common Law for the Internet. The plain, ordinary Common Law developed as the result of competing courts that issued opinions basically as advertisements of how fair and impartial they were. We could see something similar with Bitcoin arbitration. If arbitrators sign their transactions with links to and a cryptographic hash of a PDF that explains why they ruled as they did, we could see real competition in the articulation of rules. Over time, some of these articulations could come to be widely accepted and form a body of Bitcoin precedent. I look forward to reading the subsequent Restatements.

Multisignature transactions are just one of the many innovations buried deep in the Bitcoin protocol that have yet to be widely utilized. As the community matures and makes full use of the protocol, it will become more clear that Bitcoin is not just a currency but a platform for financial innovation.

6

Are Bitcoins Making Money Laundering Easier?

Katherine Mangu-Ward

Katherine Mangu-Ward is managing editor of Reason *magazine and a Future Tense Fellow at the New America Foundation.*

Many critics worry that Bitcoin will be used for money laundering. However, the truth is that most money laundering is still done through cash, which remains much harder to trace than Bitcoin. In addition, money laundering is a relatively recent crime, used by the government to prosecute illegal actions without other victims. It is mostly used in the drug war, which should be ratcheted down anyway. Bitcoin offers many advantages, and it shouldn't be legislated out of existence because of imaginary dangers.

A new protocol for keeping digital ledgers in a decentralized form doesn't exactly sound like the stuff of front-page headlines, dramatic press conferences, or televised congressional hearings. It barely sounds exciting enough to merit an afternoon breakout session at a conference of certified public accountants.

Anti-Bitcoin Freakouts

But despite its nerdy roots, bitcoin, also sometimes referred to by the much sexier description "digital cryptocurrency," seems to have a way of grabbing attention. That's probably because you can't get too far into any discussion of bitcoin before someone starts fretting about "money laundering" or talking about how absolutely everyone is buying drugs, guns, and who knows what else with this newfangled digital dough.

In 2011, New York Sen. Chuck Schumer, set the gold standard for anti-bitcoin freakouts, calling bitcoin "an online form of money laundering used to disguise the source of money, and to disguise who's both selling and buying the drug." Never one to opt for understatement or worry about technical details, Schumer also declared that bitcoin transactions on the now-shuttered Silk Road site—where people could indeed purchase illegal drugs with relative impunity, thanks to bitcoin and (more importantly) the anonymity-producing Tor network—were "more brazen than anything else by lightyears."

There have also been some high profile arrests of pleasingly scruffy-looking characters to keep interest piqued. Last week, BitInstant CEO Charlie Shrem was charged with money laundering. It looks like Shrem was working with Robert Faiella, whom he knew only by his username BTCKing, to help customers convert dollars to bitcoins for use on Silk Road. According to the Financial Crimes Enforcement Network (FinCEN), BitInstant is a payment company, so it is legally required to record and report information about its customers, particularly potentially shady dealings. Shrem, who was also on the board of the semi-official spokesorganization for the ownerless cryptocurrency, the Bitcoin Foundation, did no such reporting.

[Money laundering] laws are really about having something to throw at organized crime when other charges won't stick.

Similar money laundering charges shut down the shady sites Liberty Reserve and eGold last year. Operators of those sites argued that they should be exempt from money laundering laws since they were payment sites, not money transmitters. The feds thought otherwise.

It's not just big dogs who have attracted the attention of federal regulators. Mike Caldwell had a small online business producing physical coins engraved with a private key that could be used to unlock digital bitcoins. Late last year, he got an alarming letter from FinCEN and ceased operations. Apparently even his modest outfit fit the definition of a money transmitting firm, since he briefly held the actual value of his clients' bitcoins during the process. He has since rejiggered his product to skip that step and hopes Casascius Coins will be back in business soon.

Is Money Laundering a Crime?

The Cato Institute's Jim Harper told me in an email that money laundering "is a crime of pretty recent vintage, invented because other crimes like drug dealing have no complainants, which makes them hard to discover and prosecute." He suggests we think of money laundering as the crime of "resisting the use of money for surveillance" and remain skeptical in the face of hysteria.

He's right. Banks have been subject to some reporting requirements since the 1970s, but it wasn't until 1986 that the Money Laundering Control Act made handling dirty money a criminal act. The laws are tricky, since they require anyone who handles money to develop theories about where that money came from and why their customers are moving their money in certain ways. But a quick survey of the "specified unlawful activities" that can throw off dirty money shows just what you'd expect—drug money looms large, suggesting that the laws are really about having something to throw at organized crime when other charges won't stick. So will the world's criminals be turning to bitcoins to conceal their ill-gotten gains? One sign that Schumer and others may be barking up the wrong series of tubes is that the regulators themselves don't seem terribly concerned about that prospect. In November, the Senate's Homeland Security and Governmental Affairs Committee held a hearing, at which regulators repeatedly rebuffed efforts by senators to suggest that they might need the legislature to give them more power. An unusual sight in Washington, to say the least.

FinCEN director Jennifer Shasky Calvery, who is more or less in charge of stopping money laundering in the United States, made a list of the reasons why "illicit actors" might like virtual currencies. Her list includes the fact bitcoin and other virtual currencies are "relatively simple for the user to navigate," "may have low fees," are "accessible across the globe with a simple Internet connection," "can be used both to store value and make international transfers of value," "is generally secure," feature "irrevocable transactions," and have "no administrator to maintain information on users."

Bitcoin may continue to be unappealing for criminals due to the public nature of the ledger—every bitcoin transaction is made public, albeit pseudonymously.

Kind of sounds like an advertisement for bitcoin, no? She acknowledged that many of these reasons are appealing to legit users as well and notes that not all innovation in money transmission is pernicious, citing online banking and prepaid debit cards as beneficial for a wide variety of users. She also expressed confidence that no new laws are needed to catch bad actors, even if they choose to do business in bitcoin.

Cash Is Still Best

Later in the same hearing, Edward Lowery, a special agent with the Secret Service, takes on the question with a hint of a smirk and a raised eyebrow. "High level international cybercriminals," he says of his experience, "have not by-and-large gravitated to the peer-to-peer cryptocurrency, such as bitcoin."

Instead, they prefer "centralized digital currency" that is based somewhere with looser regulations and lazier enforcement.

And as Shasky Calvery notes off the cuff during the question and answer portion of the hearing: "Cash is probably still the best medium for laundering money." For now, regulators are being surprisingly restrained in their approach to bitcoin. As Cato's Harper notes, bitcoin may continue to be unappealing for criminals due to the public nature of the ledger—every bitcoin transaction is made public, albeit pseudonymously. "But even if it were" an effective tool for money laundering, he says, "you start to ask yourself: Are we going to forgo financial innovation and its massive consumer benefits—life, health, human welfare of all kinds—to prop up the drug war?"

Money laundering is the process of throwing needles into a haystack. The idea is to lose dirty cash in a jumble of legitimate transactions. About $8 billion worth of transactions were conducted in bitcoin from October 2012 to October 2013. During 2012, Bank of America processes $244.4 trillion in wire transfers and PayPal processed $145 billion. The bitcoin haystack just isn't big enough or messy enough to be a useful place to launder money right now. A better option: cash-heavy businesses, such as casinos or—yes—laundromats.

7

The Mt. Gox Disaster Has Seriously Damaged Bitcoin

Michael Lewis

Michael Lewis is a staff reporter in the Toronto Star*'s business section covering technology issues, including IT, mobile computing, and telecommunications.*

The collapse of Bitcoin exchange Mt. Gox and the hacking theft of around $300 million have shown the weaknesses and insecurity of Bitcoin. The incident demonstrates that Bitcoin can be very unsafe, and that those who trade in it or use exchanges expose themselves to serious risks. The incident seems likely to damage faith in Bitcoin and perhaps to seriously harm the currency.

The collapse of a major bitcoin exchange in Japan has some experts warning of hastened regulation of virtual currency among global governments.

The reported hacking theft of 740,000 bitcoins (more than $300 million U.S.) from the exchange "is just the latest in the long line of unrecoverable thefts," said financial analyst Peter Leeds in an email.

Wide-Ranging Effects

"The network was always at risk, but now with a sudden drop of over 20 per cent (in the virtual currency's value) a tipping point is being approached which would derail the entire system."

Michael Lewis, "'The End of Bitcoin'? Major Online Exchange Mt. Gox Goes Bust," *Toronto Star*, February 25, 2014. Copyright © 2014 Toronto Star Newspapers Ltd. All rights reserved. Reproduced with permission.

Leeds said the demise of the Tokyo-based bitcoin trader Mt. Gox will force complacent governments to cobble new regulation, as well as discourage individuals from using the "crypto-currency."

But Joseph David, the CEO of the Canadian Virtual Exchange [CVA], said he would welcome greater oversight, arguing that the system here is stable and can sustain more scrutiny to bolster public confidence.

David added that domestic virtual exchanges are subject to currency trading compliance laws under anti-laundering and anti-terrorism statues, for example. He said the CVE has conservatively confined its transactions to Canadian residents and complies with requirements including those that prohibit anonymous exchanges of Canadian currency amounting to more than $3,000 (Cdn.) per month.

David said the CVA has conducted Canadian currency and bitcoin exchange transactions valued at more than $73 million over three years and has 34,000 customers. He said adoption is surging and sales of bitcoins advanced after the collapse in Japan triggered the currency's drop in value.

The collapse of Mt. Gox, following months of secret catastrophic losses, serves as a warning to those who buy and trade in the popular digital currency.

David said the Canadian exchange enjoyed a trading surge after the Mt. Gox theft triggered a decline in the currency's value to about $470 (U.S.) from $550 over several hours.

On bitcoin exchanges, the currency's value has fallen to about $470 from $550 in the past few hours. The figure was already down more than 50 per cent on the price of $1,200 per bitcoin reached on Mt. Gox three months ago.

"We've been criticized for not going international but that's how we've avoided a lot of problems with security,"

David said. "We are completely stable and we are not affected by these issues. We as a community just want Mt. Gox to go away."

The head of the Bitcoin Alliance of Canada says the collapse of Mt. Gox, following months of secret catastrophic losses, serves as a warning to those who buy and trade in the popular digital currency.

Lessons Learned

Anthony Di Iorio, the executive director at the non-profit organization, advises that the lesson to be learned is that large amounts of Bitcoins should not be left on any exchange or service due to possible security risks.

"The great thing about Bitcoin is that you can be your own bank and nobody has access to your funds," he said Tuesday.

"But if you are putting them in an exchange, and you're buying and selling, you have to have them stored there at least for a small amount of time."

The risk with leaving money languishing with a third-party is that if the site shuts down, the investment can be gone with it.

The website of Mt. Gox was returning a blank page Tuesday following the resignation Sunday of Mt. Gox CEO Mark Karpeles from the board of the Bitcoin Foundation, a group seeking legitimacy for the currency, and a withdrawal ban imposed at the exchange earlier this month.

Prominent members of the bitcoin community, meanwhile—including San Francisco-based wallet service Coinbase and Chinese exchange BTC China—sought to shore up confidence in the currency in a statement that said Mt. Gox abused users' trust.

"As with any new industry, there are certain bad actors that need to be weeded out, and that is what we are seeing today," their joint statement said.

Documents purportedly leaked from the company lay out the scale of the problem. An 11-page "Crisis Strategy Draft" published on the blog of entrepreneur and bitcoin enthusiast Ryan Selkis says that 740,000 Bitcoins are missing from Mt. Gox.

"At the risk of appearing hyperbolic, this could be the end of bitcoin, at least for most of the public," the draft said.

The scandal may cost bitcoin enthusiasts dear.

At the Tokyo office tower housing Mt. Gox, bitcoin trader Kolin Burgess said he had picketed the building since Feb. 14 [2014] after flying in from London, hoping to get back $320,000 he has tied up in bitcoins with Mt. Gox.

Trust Shaken

"I may have lost all of my money," said Burgess, next to placards asking if Mt. Gox is bankrupt. "It hasn't shaken my trust in bitcoin, but it has shaken my trust in bitcoin exchanges."

Mt. Gox CEO Karpeles did not immediately return several messages seeking comment. A security officer at the office tower said no one from Mt. Gox was in the building. Tibbane, an Internet company that Karpeles is CEO of, still has its name listed on the building's directory.

"I have no idea" where they are, said Burgess, the trader. "I'm both annoyed and worried."

Even if Mt. Gox doesn't drag bitcoin down with it, there's fear that the exchange's demise will push officials to take an even more skeptical stance.

The disappearance of Mt. Gox could be fatal for bitcoin, which was started in 2009 as a currency free from government controls. Bitcoin's boosters say the currency's design make it impossible to counterfeit and difficult to manipulate, and the virtual money has won an eclectic mix of die-hard fans, including libertarians, tech enthusiasts and adventurous investors.

But the currency has struggled to shake off its associations with criminality, particularly its role in powering the now-defunct online drug marketplace Silk Road. Only last month another member of the Bitcoin Foundation, Vice Chairman Charlie Shrem, was arrested at New York's Kennedy Airport on charges of money laundering.

Authorities have been taking an increasingly hard look at bitcoin and related virtual currencies including Litecoin, Namecoin, Ripple, and countless others. Some countries, including Russia, have effectively banned the currency. In other jurisdictions, authorities are weighing whether to try to tame the marketplace through licences or other mechanisms.

Even if Mt. Gox doesn't drag bitcoin down with it, there's fear that the exchange's demise will push officials to take an even more skeptical stance.

"I think this is disastrous from a (regulatory) standpoint," Selkis, the enthusiast, said in a message posted to Twitter. "The hammer will now come down hard."

Bitcoin was started in 2009 as an unregulated currency, free of control from governments and central banks. There are an estimated 21 million bitcoins in circulation, but statistics on their usage are unavailable.

Some countries, including Russia, have effectively banned the currency. It is not recognized as legal tender by the Bank of Canada and, in other jurisdictions, authorities are weighing whether to try to tame the marketplace through licenses or other mechanisms.

To access bitcoin, users set up and manage a digital wallet and can process transactions using their smartphones.

The digital currency is seen as more convenient than other forms of payments because they can be sent directly and instantly from one person to another and do not include processing and other fees usually charged by banks or third parties.

Lisa Kramer, an associate finance professor in Toronto, said the shut down is not a surprise because Mt. Gox has been dealing with serious security issues for several months, including users recently being banned from making withdrawals.

"Bitcoin has been operating in limbo for some time. The writing has been on the wall," said Lisa Kramer, with the Rotman School of Management at the University of Toronto.

"A lot of economists had been predicting that Bitcoins days are numbered."

Kramer said people use Bitcoin due to convenience and ease, and Mt. Gox shows that these reasons may no longer apply.

"A centre point of any currency's existence is that users have faith in its stability as a medium of exchange. When you need your currency, it needs to be there for you. Mt. Gox has been having trouble obtaining their Bitcoins for some time now and now it looks like they won't get their Bitcoins at all," she said.

"This will decrease trust in Bitcoins."

8

Bitcoin Shrugs Off Mt. Gox's Death Rattle

Andy Greenberg

Andy Greenberg writes for Forbes *covering data security, privacy, and hacker culture.*

The collapse of the Mt. Gox exchange after hackers stole hundreds of millions of dollars in bitcoins has not damaged Bitcoin long-term. On the contrary, the elimination of the untrustworthy site has strengthened the Bitcoin community. The site's failure has highlighted the need for better security, but again that will only serve to improve other exchanges. There is no sign that Mt. Gox will destroy Bitcoin.

The Bitcoin community may not exactly be dancing on the grave of Mt. Gox, the oldest and once-largest cryptocurrency exchange, which officially filed for bankruptcy in Japan Friday morning. But it's happy enough to step over Gox's corpse and go about business as usual.

Bad Actors Removed

As of Friday afternoon, Bitcoin's exchange rate with the dollar remained at close to $550 according to the Coindesk price index average across the currency's exchanges, virtually the same as the currency's exchange rate a week earlier despite Mt. Gox's sudden disappearance from the web Monday and final bankruptcy announcement four days later. In fact, the currency rose more than 20% from its lowest point after Mt. Gox's vanishing act, showing signs of relief after years of suffering from the exchange's outages, hacks, and delays rather than the catastrophe some predicted after Gox's demise.

"The Bitcoin community responds well when bad actors are removed from the system," says Ezra Galston, a venture capitalist with Chicago Ventures who has considered investing in Bitcoin startups but doesn't yet hold stakes in any. "Whether the price in a year is $400, $800 or $2,000, I'm not smart enough to predict. But there doesn't seem to be a huge risk of Bitcoin not existing in a year."

The last so-called "bad actor" to be removed from the Bitcoin economy, Galston argues, was the Bitcoin-based black market for drugs known as the Silk Road, whose takedown by the FBI in early October [2013] resulted in the seizure of more than 1.5% of all Bitcoins in existence. Although the Silk Road seizure sparked an immediate 20% drop in Bitcoin's price, it quickly recovered to reach values over $1,000 per bitcoin just weeks later.

Bitcoin startups are wising up to the security measures necessary to keep thieves' hands off their coins.

Though Mt. Gox's initial signs of distress took a similar chunk out of Bitcoin over the past weeks, shaving hundreds of dollars off its price, the worst is over, says Andreas Antonopoulos, chief security officer of Bitcoin wallet Blockchain.info. "The market had pretty much priced in Gox's failure," he says. He points to new entrants in the Bitcoin industry who he believes will offer more stable exchanges, such as SecondMarket, Circle and Coinsetter. "This was an amateurish and incompetently managed company . . . it will be replaced by competent operators who run better exchanges."

In fact, Antonopoulos and others blame Mt. Gox for no less than five prior crises in Bitcoin that often had much more dramatic effects on the digital currency's value. When the exchange was first hacked in the summer of 2011, the news led to the first Bitcoin sell-off, plummeting its price from $35 to just a few dollars. Antonopoulos argues that Mt. Gox's hour-long delays in trading in April of last year was the cause of the currency's second major crash from a value of $266 to around $50. Mt. Gox's problems had become frequent enough that to be "goxed" has become a verb in Bitcoin-speak, meaning to be "fooled or trolled repeatedly" according to the Urban Dictionary.

Better Security Needed

Compared with those earlier price drops, the latest from the final death of Mt. Gox seems relatively tame. But Gox's problems still highlight real problems with Bitcoin, namely the ease with which it can be stolen from companies that don't take strict security precautions. Mt. Gox says its problems stem from a hack that made off with 850,000 Bitcoins that belonged to its users, worth more than $450 million. That reminder that Bitcoins can be stolen from an insecure vault—like any cash or commodity—no doubt played into the currency's slide from earlier in the month.

But Bitcoin startups are wising up to the security measures necessary to keep thieves' hands off their coins. Mt. Gox has been criticized for improperly safeguarding its coins in "cold storage"—the majority of its savings should have been held offline, where it would be impervious to even the most clever hacker. Instead, as my colleague Kashmir Hill points out, it seems to have held them in "lukewarm storage" that allowed the private keys to leak onto Internet-connected systems; that's not a mistake other legitimate players in the Bitcoin economy are likely to repeat.

"This has been tragic for the people who lost money, but we're putting it behind us," Antonopoulos says. "The silver lining is that we won't be goxed again."

9

Bitcoin Is Built on and Promotes Privilege and Inequality

Annie-Rose Strasser

Annie-Rose Strasser is senior editor at ThinkProgress.org.

Those who use Bitcoin are relatively wealthy white men. These users can afford to put their money in a risky currency. They also like the idea of getting rid of government interference. Other groups, like the poor, have no use for this kind of libertarian dream of freedom from government. Instead, marginalized groups need the government to intervene on their behalf to make sure they are not discriminated against in terms of banking services. Bitcoin, therefore, is a tool of the wealthy and powerful, and it will never serve the needs of the rest of society.

Every once in a while—most recently with the collapse of online exchange site Mt Gox—the world starts paying attention to Bitcoin, the hacker-project-cum-digital-currency that has garnered the love of a certain subset of people on the internet. Who are those people? According to an online poll from Simulacrum, the average user is a 32.1-year-old libertarian male. By users' accounts, those men are mostly white.

Bitcoin and White Men

Breaking that down, about 95 percent of Bitcoin users are men, about 61 percent say they're not religious, and about 44 percent describe themselves as "libertarian / anarcho-capitalist." On the last point, the political ideology of Bitcoin users is evident from the fact that the whole idea behind Bitcoin is that it segregates economic markets and currency from a country's government. Bitcoin aims to be a universal currency, connecting people "peer-to-peer" instead of through set institutions. It wants to replace our current economic system and practices in their entirety—changing the way we buy goods and distribute money. The libertarians, or anarcho-capitalists as the case may be, don't trust the government to handle their money. They're the same people who want to "end the fed."

Bitcoin users' rejection of the government reflects the luxury of being able to live well without state support, while the less advantaged desperately need a larger government role in the banking system to help them overcome deep, systemic bias.

Those libertarian tendencies are generally held by white men. "Compared to the general population," an American Values survey reported last year, "libertarians are significantly more likely to be non-Hispanic white, male, and young." Specifically, 94 percent are white, and 68 percent are men. Why does Bitcoin specifically have this demographic makeup? Well, there's a fair amount of privilege built directly into the currency: In order to buy the sometimes wildly expensive currency, Bitcoin users need to be wealthy. And they can afford to put their wealth into a currency that isn't widely accepted or even recognized. Plus, they move easily through the financial and digital space—the process of "mining" bitcoins demands it; it is all about knowing coding and decryption and how to use an exchange. The sum total of these things—advanced knowledge of computer science, wealth—are also markings of the young, white male.

The Unbanked

But they're not the only ones who are operating outside of our enshrined banking system. Other groups, the demographic opposites of the Bitcoin crowd, are doing the same. The clinical terminology for those people is the "unbanked"—they rely on informal, instead of formalized, systems of trading or borrowing capital. Why? The unbanked, comprised of women and people of color, are much more frequently turned down for auto loans, mortgages, and investment advice. Or, when they go into formalized systems, the government isn't there to protect them. Instead, they're taken advantage of by unregulated banking—unbanked households on average spend over $2,400, about 10 percent of their income, to use services like payday lending and check cashing.

So they seek options outside of the banking system as mainstream America knows it. One example is a sou-sou. Formally known as a Rotating Savings and Credit Association, and called a "min," "sub," "partner," or "sociedad" by various ethnic groups, sou-sous originated in West Africa and were brought to the United States by Caribbean and African immigrants. They're effectively community banks: A group of people put money at regular intervals into a shared fund and then at regular intervals distribute out that lump sum to one person in the group. So, for example, a group of 10 people would put in $1,000 a month, and once a month one person would receive $10,000 to do with as they please. It works simultaneously as a savings plan and a credit plan—all without interest. And sou-sou participants say that there's more accountability and obligation to the fund because you know the other people in it.

Obviously, the structures of sou-sous and Bitcoin are vastly different. Bitcoin users reject the premise of a currency backed by the government entirely, while communities of color that participate in sou-sous are simply shut out from the system that exists and still rely on our country's currency. But the question stands as to why Bitcoin doesn't reflect the ranks of the unbanked at all. Why isn't the crypto-currency of the future taking hold among communities other than the elite?

Bitcoin users' rejection of the government reflects the luxury of being able to live well without state support, while the less advantaged desperately need a larger government role in the banking system to help them overcome deep, systemic bias.

That American system of banking and government regulation has failed at points, but it's worked more often than a libertarian system would. Despite being wronged by the system again and again, women and people of color actually don't want a smaller government. They are the ones who need more institutional support, not less, to be financially successful. When payday lenders are skimming off their paychecks, they support policies like Sen. Elizabeth Warren's (D-MA) plan to turn U.S. Postal Service offices into local banks. When black and Latino people alleged that they were being denied auto loans based on their skin color, the Department of Justice and the Consumer Financial Protection Bureau stepped in to sue the bank responsible. Similarly, when gays and lesbians found they were being denied mortgages by Bank of America based on their sexual orientation, the Department of Housing and Urban Development sued, citing its own anti-discrimination protections.

The fact that Bitcoin's followers deeply oppose this sort of aggressive government action explains why their aspirations to building a universal currency aren't working. The people who most need alternatives to the current banking system are seeking policy alternatives, not libertarian stabs at undermining the state. While they might be able to find a fix to the technological problems plaguing Bitcoin and Mt Gox, that's a problem they haven't solved.

10

Bitcoin Promotes Equality and Freedom

Meghan K. Lords

Meghan K. Lords is the editor of Bitcoin Not Bombs; *she has written for* Bitcoin Magazine, Freedom's Phoenix, *and* Attack the System.

The argument that Bitcoin is only used by wealthy white men is false. In fact, Bitcoin has been used in charitable efforts to help the homeless and transfer funds cheaply to disaster areas. Bitcoin is used by those without access to banks, and also by those who have reason to distrust the state, which often oppresses marginalized communities. Bitcoin is a tool that can help push back against state power and help promote freedom and justice.

With the media frenzy in full tilt after the closing of Mt-Gox [a Bitcoin exchange that was hacked], there have been quite a few articles coming out declaring the death of bitcoin and an equal number reassuring us that it will be just fine. I won't link to the former ones because they're so painfully uninformed and rely on tired scare tactics. I have come across one article of a different vein, though, and it seeks to bring in the toxic philosophy of privilege checking as a critique against the Bitcoin community. I could wax philosophic about the specific problems with the academia class developing a divisive practice based on classist, racist, and sexist premises, but I specifically want to address the claims of the author of this piece.

Bitcoin and Charity

There's no shortage of commenters decrying the inequality of the Bitcoin community from their ivory towers, but to say Bitcoin is "by the privileged, for the privileged" is a new low. The author, Annie Rose-Strasser, claims that Bitcoin is a boy's club and cites statistics that show men dominate the sphere, but this is neither new nor compelling news. The tech field is dominated by men because more men prefer tech work than women for several reasons, similar to how more women dominate other fields such as nursing and teaching. I've argued before that these preferences are not a bad thing and believe they represent a natural division of labor that arises when you have a relatively free economy in which people are not forced into specific fields of work.

The state is standing in the way of one of the largest unbanked groups gaining financial and physical independence.

Even though men make up the majority of Bitcoiners they do not work to exclude women, people of color, or those in poverty; in fact, the fastest growing sector of the Bitcoin economy is charities—each of which equally feature women in prominent roles and some of which feature no men on their teams. I am in the unique position of being in one of these myself (Bitcoin Not Bombs) and working closely with the other ones—mainly Sean's Outpost Homeless Outreach, Fr33 Aid, and Antiwar.com. BitGive, Shire Sharing, Bitcoin100, and Good-Bits are other charities/nonprofits that also use bitcoin to help others. Bitcoin100 actually lists dozens more charities that accept bitcoin on their site, and to date the charities I have mentioned have helped thousands of people locally and globally suffering from poverty whether due to homelessness or natural disasters like the typhoon in the Philippines.

It is no longer a hypothetical theory that bitcoin can be used to help the downtrodden; it is a reality that takes place every day. Sean's Outpost Homeless Outreach has served over 50,000 meals to homeless residents in Pensacola alone and has bought a nine acre property that will be used as a safe camping space for the homeless, Bitcoin Not Bombs clothed and fed hundreds in their Hoodie the Homeless project, Fr33 Aid sent medical supplies and aid to hundreds afflicted by the typhoon in the Philippines, and Shire Sharing fed over 1,000 people Thanksgiving dinner in New Hampshire. The ability of bitcoin to be sent internationally in a matter of seconds directly to individuals in need for nearly free is ushering a new era of mutual aid and global cooperation. Strasser supplied zero evidence that bitcoin harms the poor, and it is abundantly clear that bitcoin is being used for the very things she claims it isn't used for.

Strasser makes the extremely ignorant assumption that due to this male dominance, Bitcoin users are hostile to the unbanked and other oppressed groups. You would have to be living under a rock feasting solely on anti-Bitcoin propaganda to think that Bitcoin is only about making money and oppressing the lesser privileged. In fact, Bitcoin can help the unbanked more than government agencies. You do not need a driver's license, bank, or even a place of residence to start using bitcoin. There are homeless people in Pensacola, FL who have literally used bitcoin to pull themselves out of poverty— good thing they have their home now so they can check their privilege.

The State vs. the Poor

After speaking with Jesse, one of the men featured in the *Wired* story, their biggest hurdle to getting into a home was going through the costly regulations imposed by the state. When you speak with other homeless people in Pensacola, you learn that coding regulations prevent them from living in abandoned buildings and anti-homeless camping bans prevent them from camping on secluded public property.

The state is standing in the way of one of the largest un-banked groups gaining financial and physical independence. The anti-homeless camping bans are not unique to Pensacola, and there's even an actual state representative that physically destroys the property of homeless people in Hawaii. The homeless population is being physically oppressed by the very state Strasser argues is necessary for women of color to rise out of their situations.

Now to possibly the most offensive part of the article, Strasser actually argues that women of color in particular are dependent on the current welfare state and desperately need government programs to help them. If that isn't laying the paternalism on pretty thickly, I don't know what is. I mean, really, does the author expect women to buy this garbage? "I'm so sorry the institutional racism perpetuated by the state is causing you to suffer. Here have some more state because you are woefully unprepared to help yourself."

Strasser claims that women comprise the majority of the unbanked and that unregulated financial institutions oppress them. I'm thinking she forgot about how the government she loves so much forced banks to give loans to low income individuals who could not pay them back before the housing crisis. Or, how those predatory banks that stole the income and homes of those same disadvantaged people were then bailed out by the government. But remember that time HSBC executives got jailed for financing Mexican drug cartels who killed about 19,000 people, many of which were women? Oh wait, no, they totally got away with murder.

Government in its current form isn't so much an arm of justice as it is a way to keep those with wealth in power and immune from the laws everyone else is forced to abide by. None of the regulations on the books or proposed are going to stop powerful banking interests from committing crimes on a massive scale because of the licentious relationship between banks, corporations, and government.

If we really want perspective on privilege, the global implications of an easy to use payment system must be taken into account for its efficiency in providing aid directly to people all over the world.

And how about that drug war that disproportionately jails black men for having the wrong plant? I can't imagine why there are so many struggling, single mothers who are forced to get assistance just to survive. Good thing state sponsored thugs are there to jail their partners, brothers, fathers, and children. I fail to see how Bitcoin is more threatening than the ineffective, unjust drug war and also how Strasser fails to mention this as an influencing factor in the poverty among women of color.

Bitcoin and the Ogala Lakota Nation

Strasser asks, "Why isn't the crypto-currency of the future taking hold among communities other than the elite?" Excellent question—bitcoin is. One of the most oppressed groups in this country are Native Americans. The Ogala Lakota Nation, a sovereign Native American tribe, announced interest in Bitcoin specifically because they think it can lift them out of poverty. It's not really surprising since the government has historically persecuted the Lakotas and other tribes. The Lakotas launched the BTC Oyate Initiative Project to raise awareness about Bitcoin and even designed their own cryptocurrency called Mazacoin that is now their official currency.

If we really want perspective on privilege, the global implications of an easy to use payment system must be taken into account for its efficiency in providing aid directly to people all over the world—especially disadvantaged women, many of which must raise families on low resources while their partner finds work in more economically healthy areas.

The ability for affordable and quick remittances is one of the most promising aspects of Bitcoin. There's no comparison with Bitcoin and Western Union when it comes to being a cheap, effective money transmitting system. You can't beat 1% or less transaction fees versus the 12% it takes to send money via Western Union to the poorest parts of Africa. Bitcoin Not Bombs is currently printing Bitcoin quick start guides in Spanish so that people here and across the border can use it to send money to their families back home and avoid high fees. These fees eat up a good portion of what they are able to send to their families back home (and depending on the service, the transaction can be denied), and Bitcoin eliminates these problems.

In many cases, being unbanked is a choice made by people who have been historically disenfranchised by banks, and I think it is important not to discount the distrust many still correctly have of banking institutions. Let's not forget the failure of the Freedman's Saving Bank, which was set up under Abraham Lincoln. After its failure, depositors—the majority of whom were freed slaves—did not get properly compensated for their losses. I would even say it's arguable whether the FDIC has the funds to replenish bank deposits in the instance of a modern bank run, but if you trust corrupt banks with your money I guess that's a risk people are willing to take. Bitcoin doesn't rely on trusting a third party with your money; its structure forces the individual to be their own bank. While some debate whether that is a flaw or feature, for the unbanked already used to controlling their own money independent of banks it is familiar and easy to transition into.

Those "privileged" Bitcoiners are enthusiastic about helping the unbanked get set up with Bitcoin and many spend hours assisting those curious about the protocol and currency. Knowing about the drive, mission, and concern of the individuals in the larger community specifically for the unbanked and less privileged is crucial before you can outright dismiss all Bitcoiners as selfish libertarians twirling their Monopoly man mustaches.

The entire paradigm of centralized control of finances and aid is shattered when you can send funds directly to someone in need.

The fastest way to get someone started with bitcoin is to help them open a wallet and give them a small amount. I have done this and seen it done numerous times; the community literally gives away money to anyone willing to set up a wallet. Indeed it is how many current Bitcoiners got started. And bitcoin is affordable because you don't have to buy a whole one at a time, you could buy fractions of a bitcoin depending on your budget. For those unbanked who rely on under the table paid work, Bitcoin is a great way to accept a variety of currencies and actively participate in a new economy—one which rewards bitcoin friendly businesses with consistent patronage.

Bitcoin as a payment system/network and as a currency (lowercase b) is also not necessarily trying to replace the current flawed system, as Strasser claims: "It wants to replace our current economic system and practices in their entirety—changing the way we buy goods and distribute money." My sides! So, you mean to tell me exchanging a currency for goods and services just like you can with cash, credit cards, PayPal, wire transfers, and checks is replacing the current economic system entirely? Strasser doesn't appear to have used bitcoin or she would know that it is a currency that functions just like any other method of payment, and sometimes more smoothly with less of a chance to commit fraud and steal from merchants like you can with credit cards. Right now, the Bitcoin economy functions parallel the mixed economy, but is superior in many ways.

Bitcoin Breaks Down Barriers

It's unfortunate to see such inaccurate claims about Bitcoin's ability to rectify societal inequalities because if anything Bitcoin breaks down these barriers erected between individuals by the corrupt banking institutions and government. The entire paradigm of centralized control of finances and aid is shattered when you can send funds directly to someone in need.

Millennials are another group that Bitcoin has helped; the fact that these people regardless of race or gender have made some money out of investing early in bitcoin is great news—not something to feel shame over. It's appalling that Strasser is saying these same people are somehow terrible because they narrowly escaped the financial destitution many in our generation face after going into massive debt for college degrees with little demand in a struggling economy.

Bitcoin cannot possibly be limited to only the privileged as anyone . . . can gain access to it through standard cell phones, a tool which the developing world has increasing access to.

Bitcoin should be lauded as a success story for the Millennial generation [those born between the 1980s and 2000s], and while I have not personally made massive gains like some, Bitcoin has helped me secure some financial independence as a female Millennial who was priced out of college and struggled in numerous dead end jobs for years. This is not an uncommon occurrence. . . . Not all Bitcoiners are wealthy venture capitalists; many are graduates or students faced with crippling debt whose incomes are whittled away by government programs designed to siphon money from the poor and middle classes to older generations. The class implications alone are worthy of considering when talking about Bitcoin's ability to help the disadvantaged.

The Bitcoin world is not all rainbows and roses, and yes you do have to be concerned with criminal elements. The criminals active in Bitcoin are dangerous, but concern over the 0.5% of transactions associated with black market activity is laughable compared to the destruction wreaked by even just one facet of the empire—war; the swiftest way to increase poverty worldwide. For countries torn apart by war, Bitcoin is an excellent way for people outside the conflict to give direct aid and remittances for families who aren't able to return to their countries (or conversely, escape). This function is really what makes Bitcoin disruptive—it threatens the forces that keep people enslaved by warfare.

Strasser is correct in thinking Bitcoin is dangerous; it is dangerous to war profiteers, corrupt banking institutions, unethical banking practices, usurious money transmitting services, tyrannical governments, failed foreign aid programs, and systems that keep people in poverty.

Strasser is attempting to force Bitcoin into the mold of social engineers that use buzzwords such as privilege to shame people for doing benign activities like having bitcoins. While shame no doubt has its place for dissuading harmful activities, the privilege argument against Bitcoin is incredibly weak. Privilege is simply defined as a special right, advantage, or immunity granted or available only to a particular person or group of people. Bitcoin cannot possibly be limited to only the privileged as anyone (even people in Kenya) can gain access to it through standard cell phones, a tool which the developing world has increasing access to.

I challenge Strasser and others to go beyond the thinking that Bitcoin is bad because white dudes predominantly use it and they are "bad"; it is intellectually lazy and insulting to the thousands of non-white, non-male, non-libertarian human beings that use and benefit from the use of Bitcoin every day.

The barriers to entering the Bitcoin economy are lower than getting a bank account or drivers' license making it an ideal system for the unbanked and impoverished. Social justice advocates would be keen to embrace Bitcoin with open arms as it—in real time not theoretically—is leveling the playing field and providing the most disenfranchised with opportunities previously unavailable.

11

Government Eyes Regulation of "Bitcoins"

Kavya Sukumar

Kavya Sukumar is a freelance developer-journalist and a former Microsoft engineer.

Congress is thinking about regulating Bitcoin, especially in order to try to prevent the currency from being used to finance illegal activities and money laundering. Some Bitcoin users do not want any regulation. However, many commenters and experts feel that government regulation will help legitimate the currency and make it more attractive to a broader group of users. Government regulation is necessary for Bitcoin to mature and become more widely accepted.

A Senate committee is investigating whether to establish regulations for online "virtual currencies" such as Bitcoins.

Congress and Bitcoin

Bitcoins, a widely used virtual currency, are an alternative to money online. Unlike regular money, Bitcoins are not backed by any government or company. The currency is circulated without intermediaries such as banks. This online currency, sometimes called a libertarian's dream, is not regulated or taxed. This may soon change.

The Senate Homeland Security and Government Affairs Committee sent letters last week to the Departments of Treasury, Homeland Security and other government agencies seeking details on how they oversee the use of virtual currencies, part of an investigation begun several months ago. The letters came on the heels of 22 subpoenas issued Aug. 12 by the New York Department of Financial Services to Bitcoin businesses asking questions about their policies to prevent money laundering and to provide consumer protection.

Digital currencies demand "a holistic and whole-government approach in order to understand and provide a sensible regulatory framework for their existence," committee Chairman Tom Carper, D-Del., and Sen. Tom Coburn, R-Okla., the top Republican on the committee, wrote in the letters.

The agencies have been asked to provide information to the Senate committee by the end of August [2013].

Patrick Murck, Bitcoin Foundation's general counsel, praised the committee for "proactively seeking out a productive dialog with the Bitcoin community and authorities."

Multiple attempts have been made at creating rules to oversee virtual [Bitcoin] currency operations.

Murck said, "New York is trying to set the policy for the entire country. . . . It is highly questionable if they have any jurisdiction on the issues they are trying to address."

Bitcoins can be created or "mined" on your computer. Without banks to validate transactions, the task of weeding out fraudulent transactions falls on the users. Some users called miners solve complex mathematical problems to verify transactions. They, in turn, get paid in Bitcoins for their work.

Bitcoins do not have any inherent value, but they can be exchanged for other currencies. The exchange rate for a Bitcoin, which fluctuates wildly, is nearly $120 at Mt. Gox, a Bitcoin exchange.

Bitcoin Needs Regulation

Multiple attempts have been made at creating rules to oversee virtual currency operations.

In March, the Treasury Department's Financial Crimes Enforcement Network [FinCEN] released guidelines that brought Bitcoin businesses under the same umbrella of laws as other money services businesses.

"FinCEN guidance was a starting-gun shot for the industry," said Marco Santori, a business attorney and chairman of the Bitcoin Foundation's Regulatory Affairs Committee. "It signaled that bitcoins were not contraband, but a legitimate form of value transfer."

Alan Reiner, developer of the Bitcoin software Armory, endorsed regulating Bitcoins to avoid "an unregulated system that is used mainly in black markets."

Bitcoins work by harnessing the power of computers of the users. It cannot be shutdown because there is not one owner or authority, Reiner said.

"Bitcoins put power in the hands of people who use it," Reiner said. "It is going to do to money what e-mail did to written communication."

This makes it a difficult system to control. This nearly anonymous currency fuels more than $1.2 million in sales of contraband items, including guns and drugs online, according to a study by Nicolas Christin, a researcher at Carnegie Mellon University. Transactions cannot be easily traced back to users, making it a law enforcement nightmare.

Some of the means of fighting financial crimes such as money laundering do not work on digital currencies because of the lack of a regulating authority. If the Senate investigation were to lead to regulations, private-public partnerships would be needed to detect financial crimes, Murck said.

Bradley Jansen, director of the Washington-based Center for Financial Privacy and Human Rights, said the Treasury Department's March guidance was poorly written and served only to stifle innovation. "This guidance has raised more questions than it has answered," he said. "Applying our failed banking policies on Bitcoins is a bad idea and may be the definition of insanity."

Regulations are a "necessary evil" that the Bitcoin community is willing to accept, Reiner said.

"Bitcoin cannot survive as a mainstream concept unless it has governments' approval," he said.

The economy as a whole stands to gain if the Senate committee investigation leads to clearer rules, Santori said. "Jobs will be created, tax money will be collected, customer funds will be safeguarded, and the public will benefit from a highly sophisticated and efficient value transfer system."

12

With or Without Government Regulation, Bitcoin Is Pointless

Mark Gimein

Mark Gimein is the companies and markets editor at Bloomberg .com and lead writer for the Market Now *blog and newsletter.*

After the collapse of Mt. Gox, many Bitcoin proponents are saying that government regulation would stabilize the currency and make it more attractive to a broader public. However, the entire point of Bitcoin is to provide a currency separate from government control and oversight. It is true that without government regulation Bitcoin is too volatile and risky to ever be widely used. But with government regulation it has nothing to distinguish it from government-issued currency. In short, Bitcoin has no real purpose or utility. It will inevitably disappear, with or without government regulation.

Regular readers know that I have been skeptical of Bitcoin through the whole speculative frenzy surrounding the electronic currency. Unfortunately I've also been fairly consistently wrong when it comes to the short-term outlook. Even the closing of Silk Road, the drug marketplace that was Bitcoin's most-significant non-speculative use, hasn't ended the mania.

The End Will Come

Now Mt. Gox, for several years the biggest Bitcoin exchange, has shut down. One widely circulated report claims a loss of 704,408 bitcoins (about $400 million, depending on when you're doing the counting) from thefts at the exchange. This has set off a round of stories asking if Bitcoin's future is in doubt.

I'll risk another prediction: This won't be the end of Bitcoin *yet*. That end will come, but only after a long round of efforts to keep the leaky boat afloat.

Bitcoin's future *is* in fact in doubt, but the failure of Mt. Gox is not the reason. Other Bitcoin exchanges, like Bitstamp, have already been catching up to Mt. Gox's volume because Mt. Gox was clearly not a safe place to keep your money. Over the last few months, the site was repeatedly shut down by technical problems, several times shut off withdrawals, and had money seized by U.S. regulators. It had long ago suspended withdrawals in U.S. dollars.

Bitcoin by its nature—decentralized, supra-national—cripples efforts at regulation.

In other words, a shutdown of Mt. Gox falls into the category of "So, what else is new?" If you believe that there is a need for an anonymous, decentralized electronic transaction system and are willing to live with the known risks of Bitcoin (like the fact that Bitcoins can be irretrievably lost to hacking or even computer crashes), this doesn't change much. On the contrary, if you are a caveat-emptor libertarian you might even experience some smug satisfaction in evidence that Bitcoin investing makes for a dangerous hobby. If you like the idea of a privatized currency system, you can easily chalk this up to growing pains.

If on the other hand you think (as, yes, I do) that Bitcoin has little utility for actual transactions and loses the advantages—security, reliability, traceability—of real electronic payment systems like credit cards, then the Mt. Gox fiasco hasn't changed your mind on Bitcoin either. We already knew that $1 million could be stolen, lost, or seized by the government. Why not $100 million or $400 million?

No Solution

This is the point in almost any conversation when we would be talking about whether the government should step in and regulate. Some hardcore anti-government types might be willing to accept the loss of a few tens of millions of dollars here and there to avoid the evils of government interference, but a lot of other people (i.e. most potential users) will find it unnerving that their holdings can suddenly disappear. And indeed the conversation has turned to regulation, with politicans and state regulators lining up to point out the need for rules. Even some of the true believers are getting in on the act. "Regulation is a must at this point," one investor tells *Quartz*'s Heather Timmons.

Well, wait a second: The whole point of Bitcoin was that there's no need for a central authority to regulate things, right? Truth is, the more rules get imposed on Bitcoin, the less of a purpose it has. There is no easy solution here. No, scratch that. There is *no solution at all*. Layer the apparatus of government to Bitcoin and what you've got is fiat currency without the convenience. On top of which, Bitcoin by its nature—decentralized, supra-national—cripples efforts at regulation.

That's becoming easier and easier to see. There's been plenty of talk of what governments should do about Bitcoin; we just went through a round of U.S. Senate hearings on the subject. And still, that did nothing to prevent the biggest Bitcoin exchange from going bust. What's happening with Mt. Gox doesn't demonstrate new problems with Bitcoin; those were already evident. What it demonstrates is that no one is in a position to step in and solve them.

13

The United States Should Ban Bitcoin

Joe Manchin

Joe Manchin is a United States senator from West Virginia.

Bitcoin is dangerous. It can be used to make illegal and untraceable transactions. In addition, it is deflationary, and its widespread use could damage the United States economy. Because of these issues, other countries, such as Thailand and China, have banned its use. The United States should follow suit and ban the currency before it grows more influential or widespread enough to do real harm to the country.

Today, U.S. Senator Joe Manchin (D-W.Va.) sent a letter to federal regulators seeking a ban on Bitcoin, the virtual currency that is unregulated and unstable, and has been used in illicit activity, including drug trafficking and money laundering. Senator Manchin expressed concerns about the negative effect Bitcoin could have on America's economy if this crypto-currency remains unregulated. The letter was sent to Secretary Lew, Chairwoman Yellen, Commissioner Curry, Acting Chairman Wetjen, Chairman Gruenberg, and Chairwoman White.

Please read the full text of Senator Manchin's letter below.

Dangers of Bitcoin

Dear Secretary Lew, Chairwoman Yellen, Commissioner Curry, Acting Chairman Wetjen, Chairman Gruenberg, Chairwoman White:

Joe Manchin, "Manchin Demands Federal Regulators Ban Bitcoin," Press Release, February 26, 2014. www.senate.gov. Public Domain.

I write today to express my concerns about Bitcoin. This virtual currency is currently unregulated and has allowed users to participate in illicit activity, while also being highly unstable and disruptive to our economy. For the reasons outlined below, I urge regulators to take appropriate action to limit the abilities of this highly unstable currency.

By way of background, Bitcoin is a crypto-currency that has gained notoriety in recent months due to its rising exchange value and relation to illegal transactions. Each Bitcoin is defined by a public address and a private key, thus Bitcoin is not only a token of value but also a method for transferring that value. It also means that Bitcoin provides a unique digital fingerprint, which allows for anonymous and irreversible transactions.

The very features that make Bitcoin attractive to some also attract criminals who are able to disguise their actions from law enforcement. Due to Bitcoin's anonymity, the virtual market has been extremely susceptible to hackers and scam artists stealing millions from Bitcoins users. Anonymity combined with Bitcoin's ability to finalize transactions quickly, makes it very difficult, if not impossible, to reverse fraudulent transactions.

Spending Bitcoin now will cost you many orders of wealth in the future. This flaw makes Bitcoin's value to the U.S. economy suspect, if not outright detrimental.

Bitcoin has also become a haven for individuals to buy black market items. Individuals are able to anonymously purchase items such as drugs and weapons illegally. I have already written to regulators once on the now-closed Silkroad, which operated for years in supplying drugs and other black market items to criminals, thanks in large part to the creation of Bitcoin.

Ban Bitcoin

That is why more than a handful of countries, and their banking systems, have cautioned against the use of Bitcoin. Indeed, it has been banned in two different countries—Thailand and China—and South Korea stated that it will not recognize Bitcoin as a legitimate currency. Several other countries, including the European Union, have issued warnings to Bitcoin users as their respective governments consider options for regulating or banning its use entirely. While it is disappointing that the world leader and epicenter of the banking industry will only follow suit instead of making policy, it is high time that the United States heed our allies' warnings. I am most concerned that as Bitcoin is inevitably banned in other countries, Americans will be left holding the bag on a valueless currency.

Our foreign counterparts have already understood the wide range of problems even with Bitcoin's legitimate uses—from its significant price fluctuations to its deflationary nature. Just last week, Bitcoin prices plunged after the currency's major exchange, Mt. Gox, experienced technical issues. Two days ago, this exchange took its website down and is no longer even accessible. This was not a unique event; news of plummeting or skyrocketing Bitcoin prices is almost a weekly occurrence. In addition, its deflationary trends [the money increases in value, meaning each Bitcoin can buy more goods] ensure that only speculators, such as so-called "Bitcoin miners," will benefit from possessing the virtual currency. There is no doubt average American consumers stand to lose by transacting in Bitcoin. As of December 2013, the Consumer Price Index (CPI) shows 1.3% inflation, while a recent media report indicated Bitcoin CPI has 98% deflation. In other words, spending Bitcoin now will cost you many orders of wealth in the future. This flaw makes Bitcoin's value to the U.S. economy suspect, if not outright detrimental.

The clear ends of Bitcoin for either transacting in illegal goods and services or speculative gambling make me weary of its use. The Senate Homeland Security and Governmental Affairs Committee issued a report just this month stating, "There is widespread concern about the Bitcoin system's possible impact on national currencies, its potential for criminal misuse, and the implications of its use for taxation." Before the U.S. gets too far behind the curve on this important topic, I urge the regulators to work together, act quickly, and prohibit this dangerous currency from harming hard-working Americans.

Sincerely,

U.S. Joe Manchin III

United States Senator

Organizations to Contact

The editors have compiled the following list of organizations concerned with the issues debated in this book. The descriptions are derived from materials provided by the organizations. All have publications or information available for interested readers. The list was compiled on the date of publication of the present volume; the information provided here may change. Be aware that many organizations take several weeks or longer to respond to inquiries, so allow as much time as possible.

American Enterprise Institute (AEI)

1150 Seventeenth St. NW, Washington, DC   20036
(202) 862-5800 • fax: (202) 862-7177
website: www.aei.org

The American Enterprise Institute (AEI) is a privately funded organization dedicated to research and education on issues of government, politics, economics, and social welfare. Its purposes are to defend the principles and improve the institutions of American freedom and democratic capitalism, including limited government and private enterprise. AEI publishes books, and its website includes numerous articles and policy papers on economic issues, such as "Making Sense of Bitcoin."

Bitcoin Foundation

e-mail: hello@bitcoinfoundation.org
website: www.bitcoinfoundation.org

The Bitcoin Foundation is devoted to helping people exchange resources and ideas more freely and to help Bitcoin deliver on its potential. It works to standardize Bitcoin, to make Bitcoin more secure, and to increase public awareness and understanding of Bitcoin. Its website includes a blog with news and information about Bitcoin and an online forum in which individuals can discuss issues related to Bitcoin.

Bitcoin Institute

e-mail: info@bitcoininstitute.org
website: www.bitcoininstitute.org

The Bitcoin Institute is a nonprofit think tank devoted to independent research on cryptocurrencies and their economic effects. It seeks to promote global acceptance of cryptocurrencies and to improve general understanding of how such currencies work. It also promotes research into cryptocurrencies and supports worldwide initiatives for the advancement and adoption of cryptocurrencies. The Institute's website includes access to research for members and a discussion of initiatives it supports.

Board of Governors of the Federal Reserve System

20th St. and Constitution Ave. NW, Washington, DC   20551
(202) 452-3000
website: www.federalreserve.gov

The Board of Governors of the Federal Reserve System oversees the Federal Reserve, or central bank, of the United States. The Federal Reserve was founded by Congress in 1913 to provide the nation with a safer, more flexible, and more stable monetary and financial system. The Board produces publications for specialists, such as *International Journal of Central Banking*, as well as consumer-oriented publications, such as *Consumer's Guide to Mortgage Refinancing*.

Brookings Institution

1775 Massachusetts Ave. NW, Washington, DC   20036
(202) 797-6000 • fax: (202) 797-6004
e-mail: Communications@brookings.edu
website: www.brookings.edu

The Brookings Institution is a private nonprofit organization devoted to conducting independent research, including economy research, and developing innovative policy solutions. Brookings's goal is to provide high-quality analysis and recommendations for policy makers on the full range of challenges facing an increasingly interdependent world. The Institution publishes books on economic matters, such as *Budgeting for Hard Power*, as well as numerous policy papers and reports available through its website.

Cato Institute

1000 Massachusetts Ave. NW, Washington, DC   20001-5403
(202) 842-0200 • fax: (202) 842-3490
website: www.cato.org

The Cato Institute is a libertarian public policy research foundation dedicated to increasing the understanding of public policies based on the principles of limited government, free markets, individual liberty, and peace. It publishes the triennial *Cato Journal*, the periodic *Cato Policy Analysis*, and a bimonthly newsletter, *Cato Policy Review*. The Institute's website also includes such articles as "What Is the Value of Bitcoin" and "Bitcoin Rides High on the Hill."

Council on Foreign Relations (CFR)

58 E. 68th St., New York, NY   10021
(212) 434-9400 • fax: (212) 434-9800
e-mail: communications@cfr.org
website: www.cfr.org

The Council on Foreign Relations (CFR) researches the international aspects of American economic and political policies. Its website includes numerous papers and articles on economic issues, including ones on Bitcoin, such as "Bitcoin: Questions, Answers and Analysis of Legal Issues" and "Can Bitcoin Go Mainstream?"

Ludwig von Mises Institute

518 West Magnolia Ave., Auburn, AL   36832-4501
(334) 321-2100 • fax: (334) 321-2119
e-mail: contact@mises.org
website: www.mises.org

The Ludwig von Mises Institute is a research and educational center devoted to libertarian politics and the Austrian School of economics (which is strongly opposed to loose money policies and inflation). The Mises Institute provides educational materials, conferences, media, and literature to educate the public about the importance of the market economy and sound money, and the dangers of government intervention. Its website includes numerous posts on Bitcoin, including "Bitcoin: Money of the Future or Old-Fashioned Bubble?" and "The Bitcoin Money Myth."

US Department of the Treasury

1500 Pennsylvania Ave. NW, Washington, DC   20220
(202) 622-2000 • fax: (202) 622-6415
website: www.treasury.gov

The US Department of the Treasury is the executive agency responsible for promoting economic prosperity and ensuring the financial security of the United States. The Department of the Treasury operates and maintains systems that are critical to the nation's financial infrastructure, such as the production of coin and currency, the disbursement of payments to the American public, revenue collection, and the borrowing of funds necessary to run the federal government. Its website includes a wide array of posts and articles describing financial issues and departmental functions.

The World Bank

1818 H St. NW, Washington, DC   20433
(202) 473-1000 • fax: (202) 477-6391
e-mail: pic@worldbank.org
website: www.worldbank.org

The World Bank provides monetary assistance to developing countries worldwide in the form of low-interest loans. The money provided is intended to aid these countries in developing their economies and social and political infrastructures in order to reduce poverty on a global level. Its website includes many articles about policy and financial issues, including the article "Bitcoin vs. Electronic Money."

Bibliography

Books

Susan W. Brenner — *Cybercrime: Criminal Threats from Cyberspace.* Santa Barbara, CA: Praeger, 2010.

Brett Combs and Tom Mitsoff — *Bitcoin Decoded: Bitcoin Beginner's Guide to Mining and Strategies to Make Money with Cryptocurrencies.* Whitesboro, TX: Propellerhead Marketing Group, 2014.

James Cox — *Bitcoin and Digital Currencies: The New World of Money and Freedom.* Baltimore: Laissez Faire Books, 2013.

Brian Doherty — *Radicals for Capitalism: A Freewheeling History of the Modern American Libertarian Movement.* New York: PublicAffairs, 2009.

Bernard Lietaer and Jacqui Dunne — *Rethinking Money: How New Currencies Turn Scarcity Into Prosperity.* San Francisco: Berrett-Koehler Publishers, 2013.

Tibor R. Machan and Craig Duncan — *Libertarianism: For and Against.* Lanham, MD: Rowman & Littlefield, 2013.

John Madinger — *Money Laundering: A Guide for Criminal Investigators,* 3rd ed. Boca Raton, FL: CRC Press, 2011.

Robert W. McChesney — *Digital Disconnect: How Capitalism Is Turning the Internet Against Democracy*. New York: New Press, 2013.

Philip Mulan — *The Digital Currency Challenge: Shaping Online Payment Systems Through U.S. Financial Regulations*. Hampshire, UK: Palgrave Pivot, 2013.

Sam Patterson — *Bitcoin Beginner: A Step-by-Step Guide to Buying, Selling and Investing in Bitcoins*. Charleston, WV: Better Life Publishing, 2013.

Daniel Pinchback and Ken Jordan, eds. — *What Comes After Money?: Essays from Reality Sandwich on Transforming Currency and Community*. Berkeley, CA: Evolver, 2011.

Peter Reuter — *Chasing Dirty Money: Progress on Anti-Money Laundering*. Washington, DC: Institute for International Economics, 2004.

Jonathan E. Turner — *Money Laundering Prevention: Deterring, Detecting, and Resolving Financial Fraud*. Hoboken, NJ: Wiley, 2011.

Jack Weatherford — *The History of Money*. New York: Three Rivers Press, 2009.

Majid Yar — *Cybercrime and Society*, 2nd ed. Thousand Oaks, CA: Sage Publications, 2013.

Periodicals and Internet Sources

Bloomberg   "Explaining Bitcoin Without Buzzwords," April 15, 2013. www.go.bloomberg.com.

Jon Brodkin   "'Bank' That Claimed to Solve Bitcoin's Security Problem Robbed, Shuts Down," *Ars Technica*, March 4, 2010. www.arstechnica.com.

Brian Doherty   "If It Ain't Dead, It Should Be Because It's All About 'White Privilege,'" *Reason*, February 27, 2014. www.reason.com.

Economist   "After Mt. Gox: Bitconned," March 5, 2014.

Economist   "Digital Money: The Bitcoin Bubble," November 30, 2013.

Dan Kaminsky   "Let's Cut Through the Bitcoin Hype: A Hacker-Entrepreneur's Take," *Wired*, May 3, 2013.

Paul Krugman   "Bitcoin Is Evil," *New York Times*, December 28, 2013. www.krugman.blogs.nytimes.com.

Timothy Lee   "Feds Charge Bitcoin Start-up Founder with Money Laundering," *Washington Post*, January 27, 2014.

Andrew Leonard   "Bitcoin's Amazingly Bad, but Kind of Great, Week," *Salon*, February 7, 2014. www.salon.com.

Annie Lowrey	"My Money Is Cooler than Yours," *Slate*, May 18, 2011. www.slate.com.
Alex Pearlman	"Should We Celebrate South Station's Bitcoin ATM?," Boston.com, February 19, 2014.
Paula Rosenblum	"Bitcoin: The Currency of the Future?," *Forbes*, January 27, 2014.
Matthew J. Schwartz	"Mt. Gox Bitcoin Meltdown: What Went Wrong," *Information Week*, March 3, 2014. www.information week.com.
Hiroko Tabuchi	"Japan Said to Be Ready to Impose Bitcoin Rules," *New York Times*, March 5, 2014. www.dealbook .nytimes.com.
Saumya Vaishampayan	"Virtual Currency to Remain, but Is Bitcoin the Future?," *Market Watch*, March 5, 2014. www.marketwatch .com.
Verge	"The Coin Prince: Inside Bitcoin's First Big Money-Laundering Scandal," February 4, 2014. www.theverge.com.
Joe Weisenthal	"I'm Changing My Mind About Bitcoin," *Business Insider*, December 1, 2013. www.businessinsider.com.
Roger Wu	"Why We Accept Bitcoin," *Forbes*, February 13, 2014.

Matthew Yglesias   "Why I Haven't Changed My Mind About Bitcoin," *Slate*, December 2, 2013. www.slate.com.

Index